ASSERTIVE DISCIPLINE

Elementary Materials Workbook
Grades K -6

Lee Canter
with
Marlene Canter

Canter and Associates, Inc.
Santa Monica, California

Printed in the United States of America

ISBN: 0-9608978-6-0

First Printing December 1984

Editorial Staff
    Kathy Winberry
    Barbara Schadlow

Art Director
    Kris Kegg

Table of Contents

Introduction
Section One:
How to Develop a Classroom Assertive Discipline Plan

Section Two:
Reproducibles

Section Three:
How to Develop a Schoolwide Assertive Discipline Plan

Introduction

Being a teacher in an elementary classroom is a very challenging job. Students today present many more problems than they did in the 50's, 60's and 70's. In order to deal with these problems and teach effectively, you must incorporate a Discipline Plan into your regular curriculum plans.

Assertive Discipline helps you develop the necessary skills for establishing a systematic way of dealing with the misbehavior of today's students. Underlying the Assertive Discipline approach is the following take-charge attitude: The teacher is the boss in the classroom. No student has the right to stop a teacher from teaching or another student from learning.

The theory behind Assertive Discipline and the guidelines for developing a Discipline Plan can be found in the text *Assertive Discipline — A Take-Charge Approach for Today's Educator* by Lee Canter with Marlene Canter. The *Elementary Resource Materials Workbook, K-6,* was designed to be used hand-in-hand with the text. After you have read *Assertive Discipline,* use this Workbook to help you formulate a plan that is tailored to your particular teaching situation and style.

The first section of the Workbook gives the individual teacher guidelines for establishing an effective Classroom Discipline Plan geared to situations that occur within the classroom.

The second section discusses the Schoolwide Discipline Plan and how to handle problems in the common areas of the school.

As you read each section, keep in mind that the key to effective discipline is balancing your disciplinary actions with frequent positive support of students' commendable and appropriate behavior. Children need to know that besides disciplining them, you will acknowledge them when they do behave. They need and like positive reinforcement — all people do!

Also vital to solving discipline problems is *consistency.* You, the educator, must never let up with your expectations and standards. Your students need to know that *every single time* they misbehave, they will be provided with a consequence. If you remain consistent in your efforts and determined in your attitude, you will be able to go ahead and do what you do best — teach!

SECTION ONE

How to Develop a Classroom Assertive Discipline Plan

The goal in developing a Classroom Assertive Discipline Plan is to have a fair and consistent way in which to deal with all students who misbehave, thereby creating an atmosphere conducive to teaching and allowing more time on-task for learning.

Establish Your Classroom Behavior Rules

By nature, elementary students are adventurous, spontaneous, and tireless. These characteristics can lead to behavior problems in the confines of a classroom. By disciplining elementary students you are teaching them two important concepts:

- Certain behaviors are undesirable and should be avoided.
- Other behaviors are desirable and should be repeated.

In order to know which behaviors are acceptable and are expected by you, students need very clear and firm limits.

Your first task, then, in developing a Classroom Discipline Plan, is to know exactly which behaviors you will need from your students in order to have an orderly classroom. Take time to think carefully about the behaviors you really need, then choose a **maximum of five.** These behaviors will serve as the rules for your classroom.

When determining rules be sure that they are observable. Rules such as "Bring books, notebooks, pencils to class" are observable. Rules such as "Show respect" are too vague and not observable.

The key rule that must be in effect at all times is: Students must follow your directions the first time they are given.

Examples   General Classroom Rules
- Follow directions the first time they are given.
- Be in class and seated when bell rings.
- Bring books, notebooks, pens and pencils to class.
- Raise hand to be recognized before speaking.
- Hand in all homework at the beginning of the day.
- Keep hands, feet and objects to yourself.
- Walk, don't run, at all times in the classroom.
- Keep materials in their proper areas.

Examples   Special Subject Rules
Reading
- Read silently unless otherwise directed.
- Return books to the library corner.
- Place books in neat stacks on shelves.

Music
- Do not play an instrument until told to do so.
- Be sure your instrument is properly replaced in its box when you are finished using it.
- Return music books to book shelves.

Gym
- Play all games according to the rules.
- Use equipment appropriately.
- No food or drink in the gym.
- Line up the first time the whistle blows.

 When determining rules, remember that good classroom management begins with clearly defined standards. Your students must know your expectations in order for them to behave appropriately.

CLASSROOM RULES
1 _____
2 _____
3 _____
4 _____
5 _____

REWARDS
1 _____
2 _____
3 _____
4 _____
5 _____

CONSEQUENCES
1 _____
2 _____
3 _____
4 _____
5 _____
6 _____

LEE CANTER'S ASSERTIVE DISCIPLINE

Classroom Behavior Rules

List the rules for your classroom.

1.

2.

3.

4.

5.

✓✓✓ Determine Your Classroom Disciplinary Consequences

Choosing Your Disciplinary Consequences

Once your rules are established, you must determine the disciplinary consequences you will use for students who choose to misbehave. From an early age, students need to be taught to be responsible for their actions. They need to know that in your classroom they have a choice: to follow the rules and enjoy the rewards or disregard the rules and accept the consequences.

It is important that you take the time to carefully select consequences that are appropriate for your particular teaching situation.

Guidelines
- Choose consequences *you* are comfortable using. (For example, do not keep students after school if you are not comfortable staying after school.)
- The consequences should be something the students do not like, but under no circumstances should they be physically or psychologically harmful to the students.
- The consequences should comply with school and district policy.
- Parent contact should always be included towards the end of the hierarchy.
- If sending a student to the principal is part of the hierarchy, it should be one of the last steps (except in cases of severe misbehavior).
- Choose a maximum of five consequences and list them in order of severity. These consequences will become your discipline hierarchy. The number of times a student breaks a rule in a given day will determine the consequence the student will receive.

The discipline hierarchy should also include a severe clause. This clause should state that in the case of severe misbehavior such as fighting, vandalism, defying a teacher, or stopping the class from functioning, the discipline hierarchy no longer applies. Instead, an immediate consequence will occur. Two possible severe clause consequences are:

- Send the student to the principal.
- The student receives in-school suspension. (See page 71.)

Examples   Discipline Hierarchies

1st time student breaks rule:	Name on board	= Warning
2nd time student breaks rule:	Name ✓	= 15 minutes detention after school
3rd time student breaks rule:	Name ✓✓	= 30 minutes detention after school
4th time student breaks rule:	Name ✓✓✓	= 30 minutes detention after school, call parents
5th time student breaks rule:	Name ✓✓✓✓	= 30 minutes detention after school, call parents, student sent to principal
Severe Clause:	Send to principal	

1st time student breaks rule:	Name on board	= Warning
2nd time student breaks rule:	Name ✓	= Lose 15 minutes recess
3rd time student breaks rule:	Name ✓✓	= Lose 30 minutes recess
4th time student breaks rule:	Name ✓✓✓	= Lose 30 minutes recess, call parents
5th time student breaks rule:	Name ✓✓✓✓	= Lose 30 minutes recess, call parents, send to principal
Severe Clause:	In-school suspension	

1st time student breaks rule:	Name recorded
2nd time student breaks rule:	Lunch detention
3rd time student breaks rule:	Double lunch detention
4th time student breaks rule:	Double lunch detention, call parents
5th time student breaks rule:	Double lunch detention, call parents, send to principal
Severe Clause:	Send to principal

 If you do not have access to a chalkboard (for example, in physical education class), record names and checks in a notebook or on a clipboard — any way you prefer. If students cannot see the checks you have recorded, you must tell them what the consequences are. (For example, "Linda, Rule 2" or, "Linda, that's 3 checks," or hold up the number of fingers that indicate the rule broken.)

 Remember, sending a student to the principal should be listed near the end of the hierarchy and parents should be notified 24 hours in advance of detention.

Examples   Disciplinary Consequences

- Last one out for recess
- Citation
- After-school detention (See page 69)
- Lunch detention
- Recess detention
- Letter to parents
- Phone call to parents
- Send to principal

- Yard clean-up
- Supervised lunch
- Send to another teacher's room
- Assign a designated seat
- Demerits applied to citizenship grade
- Classroom clean-up
- Miss free time

When determining your hierarchy, remember: It is not the severity but the inevitability of receiving the consequence that has impact!

Implementing Your Discipline Hierarchy

Guidelines

- Every time a student breaks one of your rules, provide him or her with a disciplinary consequence.
- The consequence should occur as soon as possible after the student misbehaves. (Be sure to notify the parents in advance before detaining a student after school.)
- Stay calm when disciplining a student.
- Make sure the student is given due process, i.e., he or she must know beforehand the consequences that will occur as a result of misbehavior.
- At the end of each day or period, erase the names and checks so the student may begin with a clean slate the next day.

If your disciplinary consequences do not work, try "tougher" ones. If you have to use the same consequence with one student three times, it means the consequence is not working. For example, if Joe has received recess detention three times in one week, your plan must be made tougher. You should drop down on the hierarchy or devise more severe consequences. "Joe, from now on, if there is one check next to your name, instead of recess detention you will receive after-school detention and I will call your parents." Be sure to inform the parents of your new plan.

When implementing your discipline hierarchy, remember that the key to your success is consistency. If you don't follow through with your consequences every time, your students will sense that you really don't mean business. Then, within a short time, they will begin breaking the rules and you will find yourself becoming frustrated and ineffective. Therefore, develop a hierarchy you are comfortable with and stick to it!

✓✓ Disciplinary Consequences

List the disciplinary consequences for your classroom.

	First time student breaks a rule
	Second time student breaks a rule
	Third time student breaks a rule
	Fourth time student breaks a rule
	Fifth time student breaks a rule
	Severe clause

Determine Your Classroom Positive Reinforcement

The next step in developing an Assertive Discipline Plan is to determine how you will positively reinforce students who do behave. ***The key to effective discipline is positive support of students' appropriate behavior.*** Negative consequences stop inappropriate behavior, but only positive consequences will change behavior. Positive reinforcement can help create a classroom that is a fun and exciting place to be.

Guidelines
- Establish positive reinforcement with which you are comfortable.
- Positive reinforcement should be something the students like.
- Students should be informed of the positive reinforcement they will receive.
- Positive reinforcement should be provided as often as possible.
- Plan ahead of time which specific appropriate behavior merits reinforcement.
- Rewards should never be taken away as punishment.

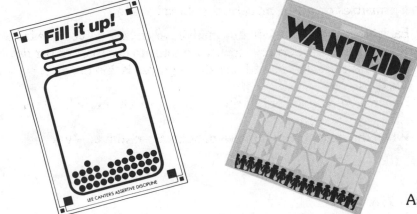

Assertive Discipline

Positively Reinforce Individual Students

The most effective reinforcer you can use is verbal praise. Focusing on what students have done right instead of what they have done wrong will help motivate them to behave.

When praising students, be very specific and mention the exact behavior you liked. Nonspecific praise such as "You did a good job today" or "Excellent work" is too vague. In order for students to repeat their good behavior, they need to know specifically what they have done right! More appropriate would be comments such as "I like the way you answered questions in class today" or "Your homework was very neatly written."

In addition to verbal reinforcement, children respond well to tangible forms of positive reinforcement. There are many positive reinforcers that elementary teachers use.

Examples   Individual Positive Reinforcers
- A positive note handed to a student, placed on his or her desk, or written on the first page of an assignment
- A positive note or call to parents
- A positive note mailed home addressed to student
- Skip a homework assignment (see page 38)
- Extra computer time
- Gift certificate from local store
- Discount at school store
- Free admission to school fair or special event
- Star or sticker placed on a chart
- Class monitor
- First in line
- Grab at Grab Bag (see page 43)
- Awards and certificates
- Lunch with teacher (see page 37)
- Free time in class
- Take home classroom pet

Remember, praise every student at least once a day and send home two positive notes per day.

Positively Reinforce the Entire Class

Marbles-in-a-jar or points are effective ways of recording classwide positive behavior. Select an activity that students can work for, then determine the number of marbles or points they must receive in a designated period of time (for example, the class will earn free time if seventy-five marbles or points are earned in three days).

Guidelines
- Each student earns at least one marble per day for appropriate behavior.
- Students with behavior problems earn three to five marbles per day.
- The class earns the reward quickly — grades K-3 in one day, grades 4-6 in one to five days.
- Never take marbles out of the jar or points off the board as a consequence for inappropriate behavior.
- When the class earns one reward, begin again with a new goal.

- Give a direction, then reinforce with marbles or points. (For example: "Take out your science books. That was quick, Steve. You just earned the class one marble.")
- Class receives the reward as soon as possible after they've earned it.

An effective way of encouraging problem students to behave is to use peer pressure. Set up the contingency that an entire class will earn a reward if a selected student(s) improves his or her behavior. (For example: If Maria is on time and brings her materials, the entire class will earn one point. When the class has earned ten points, they will receive ten minutes of free time. Or: If the entire class hands in homework every day this week, there will be no assignment on Friday.)

Examples Classroom Positive Reinforcers
- Class party (popcorn, pizza)
- No homework one night
- Field trip
- Extra recess
- Movies or cartoons
- Special lunch or dessert (see page 42)
- Free time
- Special arts and crafts projects
- Extra gym time
- Special class visitor (fireman, magician)
- Play radio in class
- Cook in class

Your disciplinary actions and positive reinforcement techniques must be used together, one balancing the other. For example, when you see Tommy misbehaving, write his name on the board. Then continue teaching while you look around for a student who is behaving. When you spot a child who is, place a marble in the jar and say, "Jeff, I like the way you're raising your hand. You just earned a marble for the class."

Remember, this balance between negative consequences and positive reinforcement is the key to successful classroom behavior management.

Free time!

Assertive Discipline

Classroom Rewards

List the rewards for your classroom.

Individual Rewards

1.

2.

3.

4.

Classwide Rewards

1.

2.

3.

4.

Present Your Classroom Discipline Plan To Administrator

Your Classroom Discipline Plan, containing rules as well as negative and positive consequences, is now complete. Your next step is to share this plan with your administrator. Having administrative support will increase the effectiveness of your plan.

Guidelines
- Complete the Teacher - Principal Worksheet on page 21.
- Share your Classroom Discipline Plan with your administrator and get his or her approval before you put the plan into effect.
- Submit the plan in writing. Include the rules, the discipline hierarchy, and positive reinforcement ideas.
- Discuss the administrator's role in your discipline hierarchy.
- Discuss what the administrator will do when a student is sent from your class to his or her office.
- Discuss what you will do when you need help and the administrator is out of the building.
- Whenever you modify your plan, share the changes with your administrator.

Teacher-Principal Worksheet

Behavior Rules For My Classroom

1. _____
2. _____
3. _____
4. _____
5. _____

Discipline Plan For My Classroom

When a student breaks a rule:

1st time _____
2nd time _____
3rd time _____
4th time _____
5th time _____
Severe clause _____

Positive Consequences I Use When My Students Behave

_____
_____
_____
_____

Students Who Require an Individualized Discipline Plan

	Name	Behavior Problem	Special Plan
1.			
2.			
3.			
4.			
5.			

Present Your Classroom Discipline Plan To Students

When your plan is complete and has been approved by your administrator, present it to your class. Discuss the details of your plan, then display a discipline poster like the one shown here.

Discipline Poster

- List your rules, consequences, and rewards.
- Laminate the poster before use so that positives can be changed weekly and adjustments to your rules and consequences can be made.
- Display the poster in a prominent location in your classroom.
- Make sure the poster is visible from all areas of the room. That way all students and visitors will be aware of your discipline standards.

Communicate Your Classroom Discipline Plan to Parents

Once your Classroom Discipline Plan is communicated to your students, send home a letter to parents. Include your rules, positive and negative consequences, and a statement of your need for parental support and a tear-off portion that parents must sign and return to you.

North Court Elementary School

482 Wilshire Street
Columbus, Ohio 43113

Dear Parent(s):

It is with pleasure that I welcome your child to my class. We can all look forward to a very exciting and rewarding school year. In order to provide my students with the excellent educational climate they deserve, I have developed the following Classroom Discipline Plan that will be in effect at all times.

Rules:

1. Follow directions.
2. Be in your seat ready to work when the bell rings.
3. Raise your hand to speak and wait to be called upon.
4. Hand in all assignments on time.
5. Keep hands, feet and objects to yourself.

If a student chooses to break a rule:

1st time:	Student's name on board	=	Warning
2nd time:	One check after name	=	Lose 15 minutes of recess
3rd time:	Two checks after name	=	Lose 30 minutes of recess
4th time:	Three checks after name	=	Lose 30 minutes of recess, parents called
5th time:	Four checks after name	=	Lose 30 minutes of recess, parents called, student sent to principal

Severe Disruption: Immediately sent to principal

Students who behave appropriately will be positively rewarded with positive notes home, praise, free time, bonus points and class parties.

It is in your child's best interest that we work together with regard to his or her education. I will thus keep you informed about your child's progress in my class.

I have already discussed this plan with your child, but would appreciate it if you would review it with him or her before signing and returning the form below.

Thank you for your support.

Sincerely,

- -

I have read your Classroom Discipline Plan and discussed it with my child.

Parent(s)/Guardian Signature _____

Child's Name _____ Date _____

Comments _____

_____

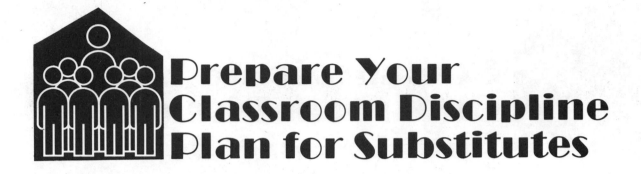

Prepare Your Classroom Discipline Plan for Substitutes

To insure consistent discipline, even when you are not present, prepare a Classroom Discipline Plan for substitutes. Make sure that a copy is left in the office. Put another copy in your plan book or tape it to the top of your desk.

From the desk of:

Dear Substitute:

The following are the guidelines for the Discipline Plan used in my classroom. Please follow them exactly, and leave me a list of students who broke the rules and a list of students who behaved properly. When I return, I will take appropriate action.

Class rules:
1. FOLLOW DIRECTIONS FIRST TIME GIVEN
2. KEEP HANDS, FEET, OBJECTS TO SELF.
3. ONE PERSON TALKS AT TIME - NO INTERRUPTING.
4. HAVE PENCILS, PAPER, BOOKS AT DESK READY TO WORK
5. SWEARING, TEASING, OBSCENE GESTURES NOT ALLOWED.

The first time a student breaks a rule, record his or her name on the board. This constitutes a warning.

The second time a student breaks a rule, record one check next to his or her name. The consequence will be
..... 15 MINUTES AFTER SCHOOL .....

The third time a student breaks a rule, record two checks. The consequence will be
..... 30 MINUTES AFTER SCHOOL .....

The fourth time a student breaks a rule, record three checks. The consequence will be
..... 30 MIN. AFTER SCHOOL + PARENTS CALLED .....

The fifth time a student breaks a rule, record four checks. The consequence will be
... 30 MIN AFTER SCHOOL, PARENTS & PRINCIPAL NOTIFIED

If a student exhibits severe misbehavior such as fighting, open defiance, or vulgar language, he or she should immediately be sent to the principal.

Students who behave will be rewarded when I return with:
.. FREE TIME IN CLASS ..
.. POSITIVE NOTES TO PARENTS ..
.. NO HOMEWORK PASSES ..

I appreciate your cooperation in following my Discipline Plan.

Sincerely,

Susan Smith

24

Substitute's Plan

Complete your plan for substitutes.

From the desk of:

Dear Substitute:

The following are the guidelines for the Discipline Plan used in my classroom. Please follow them exactly, and leave me a list of students who broke the rules and a list of students who behaved properly. When I return, I will take appropriate action.

    Class rules:

      1. ....

      2. ....

      3. ....

      4. ....

      5. ....

The first time a student breaks a rule, record his or her name on the board. This constitutes a warning.

The second time a student breaks a rule, record one check next to his or her name. The consequence will be
....

The third time a student breaks a rule, record two checks. The consequence will be
....

The fourth time a student breaks a rule, record three checks. The consequence will be
....

The fifth time a student breaks a rule, record four checks. The consequence will be
....

If a student exhibits severe misbehavior such as fighting, open defiance, or vulgar language, he or she should immediately be sent to the principal.

Students who behave will be rewarded when I return with:
....
....
....

I appreciate your cooperation in following my Discipline Plan.

Sincerely,

Plan Action for Severe Behavior Problems

The greatest number of problems confronted by a teacher in the classroom are presented by those students whose behavior is mischievous, disconcerting, disturbing and/or time-consuming. By consistently using the Assertive Discipline techniques just described, the majority of student misbehavior will be eliminated.

However, with some students who exhibit more severe problems, you may need to take stronger measures. Be aware that severe consequences should be utilized only when all else fails and that the guidelines should be strictly followed.

Effective Techniques

- Develop a Behavior Contract
- Tape Record Behavior
- Send the Student to Another Teacher's Classroom
- Have Parent Attend Class
- Send to Detention Room (see page 69)
- Send to In-School Suspension Room (see page 71)

Sending a student to either a detention room or to an in-school suspension room is probably the most effective technique for handling severe problems. Since these methods require total staff involvement they are discussed in detail in Section Three.

Develop a Behavior Contract

A Behavior Contract is an excellent aid in structuring interventions with problem students. A contract is an agreement among the teacher, principal, parent and student, and the contract is signed by all involved. (See page 53.)

Guidelines
- Determine what you want the student to do (for example, stay in seat).
- Decide what you will do if the student complies (provide points that will eventually earn the student the right to have lunch with the teacher).
- Decide what you will do if the student does not comply (the student will receive detention after school or during recess).
- Determine how long the contract will be in effect (1 week).
- The contract should be designed so that the student can earn the positive consequence quickly.

Tape Record Behavior

The teacher places a cassette tape recorder next to the disruptive student. Students will usually cease disrupting when the recorder is turned on, which is, of course, the goal of this technique. If the student disrupts while the recorder is on, play the tape for the parents and/or the principal.

Send to Another Teacher's Classroom

The disruptive student is sent to do his or her academic work in another classroom.

Guidelines
- Plan your strategy with another teacher ahead of time.
- Send the student to a well-managed classroom at a different grade level, i.e., a second-grade student to a fifth-grade class or vice versa.
- The student should sit alone in the back of the classroom doing academic work.
- The student should not take part in any class activity while there.
- At the end of the designated time period, the student is sent back to the regular classroom.

Use this method as an alternative to sending a student to the principal's office.

Have Parent Attend Class

This method is most effective for older students. The parent comes to school and sits in the classroom. The parent also accompanies the student to other rooms, including lunchroom and gym. To have the greatest effect, the parent must continue coming to school until the student shows improvement.

This method is successful because the parent sees how the child behaves in school and can then take appropriate action at home. At the same time the student feels pressure from peers about having his or her parent at school and begins to behave.

Communicate with Parents Throughout the Year

Your communication with parents should not be limited to twice-a-year routine parent-teacher conferences. To be most effective, you must establish positive communication with parents early in the school year. Then, when a problem that you cannot handle alone arises, contact the parents immediately. Do not wait until it is too late and the problem is out of hand. Use the following steps in developing a year-long plan for effective parent communication.

Communicate your standards to parents. Parents need to know your expectations if they are to support you. The first day of school send home a letter outlining your Classroom Discipline Plan. Have parents sign the letter and return it to you. (See sample, page 23.)

Positively reinforce students. Parents are accustomed to receiving only bad news from school. Sending home positive notes early in the school year will show parents you have a positive attitude towards their children. It will also increase your chances for gaining parental support if there is a problem.

Document all problems. Keep detailed records of all inappropriate behavior. (See page 56.) Doing so will enable you to relate problems to parents in a fair, nonjudgemental manner.

Be prompt. At the first sign of a problem, contact parents. Send a letter, place a phone call, or set up a conference the moment a problem arises. Do not wait until parent-teacher conferences or report card time. The problem will only get worse.

Good communication is vital to the success of your Classroom Discipline Plan. If you are having difficulty with a student and need to speak with a parent, do everything possible to reach that parent. Do not hesitate to call a parent at work. Though it may be difficult, you should not give up until you gain the parent's support.

 Remember, the child is ultimately the parents' responsibility and you, the educator, deserve parental support.

Got something to crow about . . .

Dear *Mrs. Simmons,*

Brian has completed all of his homework assignments this week — a job well done!

Mr. Davis

Teacher

A Note from Teacher . . .

Dear *Mr. and Mrs. Robinson,*

Sara has had a problem-free week on the playground. She's really working hard!

Mrs. Coates

Teacher

Document Classroom Discipline

It is vital that teachers document all student misbehavior. This recordkeeping is necessary for:

> Student record cards
> Parent/teacher/principal conferences
> Transferring students to other classes
> Referring students for special counseling
> Placement of students in continuation or
>   other special schools

At the end of the day, spend a few moments recording the names of students who misbehaved. The permanent record should include the inappropriate behavior the students engaged in and the consequences for their misbehavior.

Methods of Documentation

<u>3x5 index card</u> — alphabetically arranged in a file, one for each student

	Joanne Horn
	Grade 4, Room 202
11/3	No pencils
11/5	Running in class
11/10	Playing with water fountain
11/11	Did not hand in spelling work

Assertive Discipline

Discipline Record Sheet — one sheet per week for an entire class (see page 56)

STUDENT	DATE	RULE BROKEN	CONSEQUENCE
Mark Nelson	12/1	Yelling across room	Lose 15 minutes recess
Carol White	12/1	Did not follow directions 3X	Lose recess, parents called

Small notebook — one page for each student (can be carried to other areas throughout the school and is useful for a class with many difficult students)

	Allen Singer
10/1	10:15 A.M. — Allen & Joe had fight during reading time. I told Allen to change his seat. He refused to move and did not do any work for rest of day. I sent note home.
10/5	12:45 P.M. — Allen slapped a girl in the lunchroom. He was sent to principal's office and his mother was called.
10/9	Allen ran out of classroom for drink of water when I wasn't watching. He ran back in and collided with Sue. Allen became angry with her & pushed her to ground. Parent/teacher/principal conference is scheduled.

Classroom Discipline Plan

Assertive Discipline Analysis Worksheet

If your Assertive Discipline Plan is not working, you need to determine the reasons why. Read through this checklist to target your specific problems.

Checklist

☐ You have not communicated your expectations to the class and parents.

☐ The students like the consequences.

☐ The consequences are not provided immediately.

☐ You are not consistent in providing consequences.

☐ Your plan is not tough enough.

☐ Your plan does not apply to all students.

☐ You only follow the plan occasionally.

☐ You are not using a classwide positive reinforcement program.

☐ You do not call parents.

☐ You do not keep detailed records of student misbehavior.

If you have checked any of the above reasons, review the first section, paying particular attention to the areas that you have checked.

Sample Classroom Discipline Plan

Rules

1. Follow directions the first time they are given.
2. Keep hands, feet and objects to yourself.
3. Only one person may talk at a time. No disruptions are allowed.
4. Have pencils, papers and books at your desk ready to work.
5. Swearing, teasing or using obscene gestures is not allowed at any time.

Consequences

1st time rule is broken:	=	Name on board
2nd time rule is broken: Name ✓	=	15 minutes after school
3rd time rule is broken: Name ✓ ✓	=	30 minutes after school
4th time rule is broken: Name ✓ ✓ ✓	=	30 minutes after school, parents called
5th time rule is broken: Name ✓ ✓ ✓ ✓	=	30 minutes after school, parents called, principal notified
Severe clause	=	Send to principal immediately

Rewards

Free time in class
Positive notes to parents
No Homework passes
Special class activities

SECTION TWO

Reproducibles

Students who receive this coupon accompany the teacher to a local restaurant for lunch.

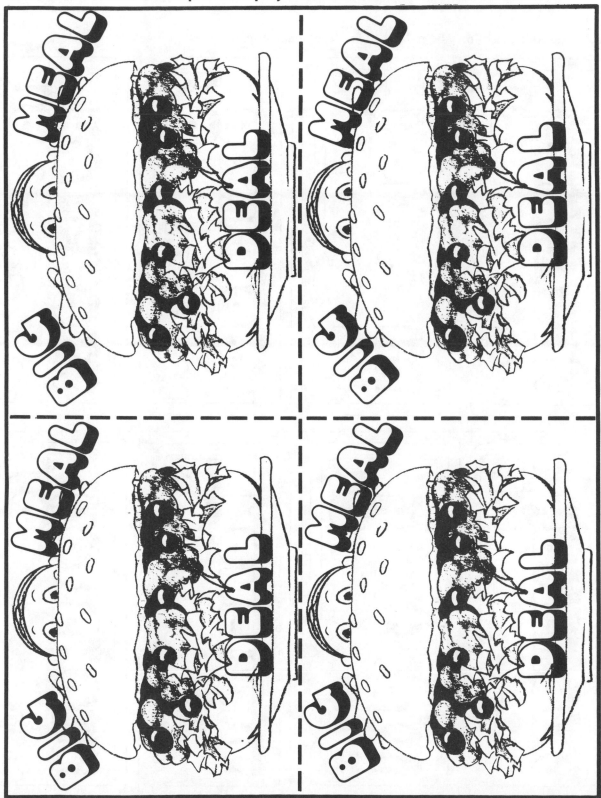

No-Homework Coupon

No-homework passes may be redeemed in place of any homework assignments in your class.

Assertive Discipline

Students may redeem these certificates for a cupful of popcorn to eat during class movies or TV programs.

King or Queen for a Day

Students who behave may wear this badge. It entitles them to be a monitor with special duties.

Assertive Discipline

These coupons entitle students to "rent" or borrow classroom games, books, pets, etc., for the weekend.

RENTAL ticket RENTAL ticket

RENTAL ticket RENTAL ticket

RENTAL ticket RENTAL ticket

RENTAL ticket RENTAL ticket

Just Desserts

Students receiving these coupons may redeem them in the cafeteria for a dessert, or you may provide a special dessert.

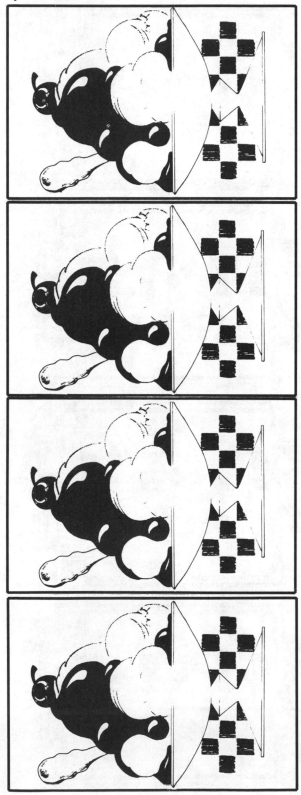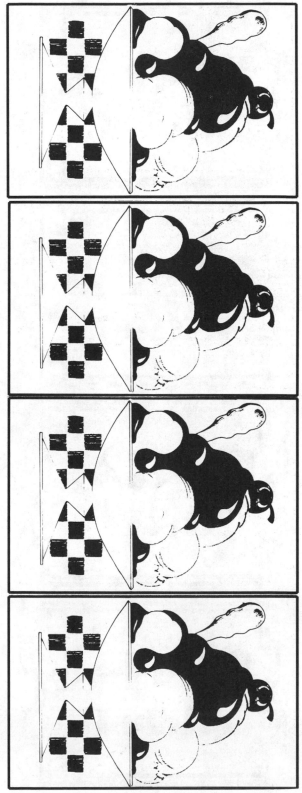

Grab Bag

Students who receive these coupons get a "grab" at the Grab Bag, which is filled with small gifts.

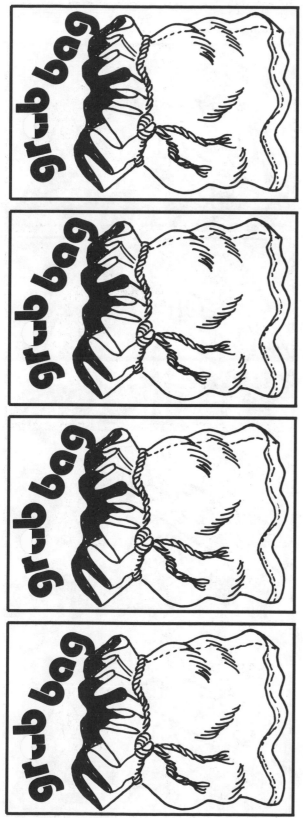

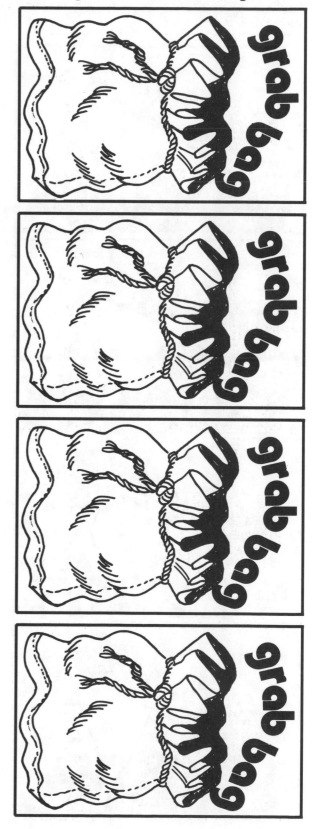

Reproducibles

Make the Grade

This coupon can be exchanged by the student for the grade of "A" on one daily quiz or homework assignment.

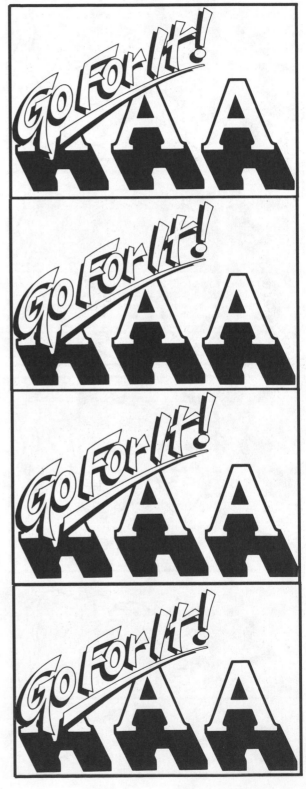

Chance Card

Students write their names on the back and deposit in a bowl or box. At the end of the month the names drawn receive rewards or small gifts.

Reproducibles

Super Kid Badge

Students who are exceptionally well behaved receive this badge to wear all day and take home to their parents.

Teacher's Award

HERE'S THE LATEST SCOOP

_____
Student

has improved
behavior at school

_____
Teacher

Egg-ceptional Award

_____
Student's Name

has demonstrated
egg-ceptional behavior!!

_____
Principal

_____
Teacher

Cafeteria Certificate

STUDENT

helps keep our cafeteria

SUPER
SUPER
CLEAN

SIGNATURE

Principal's Award

Achievement Award

presented to

_____

for outstanding behavior.

_____   _____
Date   Principal

sunnygram

Dear _____

_____

_____

_____

_____   _____
Date   Signature

_____
Date

Some News to Cheer About!

Dear

_____

_____

_____

_____
Signature

Teacher's Notes

Got something to crow about . . .

Dear

A Note from Teacher . . .

Dear

Teacher

Behavior Contract

Date _____

_____ promises to _____

_____ .

If student does as agreed, student will _____

_____ .

If student does not do as agreed, student will _____

_____ .

This contract will be in effect for _____ .

_____
Student's Signature

_____
Teacher's Signature

_____
Parent's Signature

_____
Principal's Signature

Notice of After-School Detention

NOTICE OF ASSIGNED AFTER-SCHOOL DETENTION

To the
parent(s) of _____ :

Your son/daughter has been assigned _____ minutes after-school detention in

Room _____ with _____ on _____ .

The reason for this consequence is _____

chose to be disruptive in the following manner: _____

_____

_____

_____

Please follow through at home regarding this matter.

_____   _____
SIGNED   DATE

NOTICE OF ASSIGNED AFTER-SCHOOL DETENTION

To the
parent(s) of _____ :

Your son/daughter has been assigned _____ minutes after-school detention in

Room _____ with _____ on _____ .

The reason for this consequence is _____

chose to be disruptive in the following manner: _____

_____

_____

_____

Please follow through at home regarding this matter.

_____   _____
SIGNED   DATE

Detention Room Documentation

DETENTION ROOM

STUDENT _____ DATE _____

TEACHER _____ AMOUNT OF TIME_____

WORK TO BE DONE _____

TIME IN	TIME OUT	
		SUPERVISOR'S SIGNATURE

COMMENTS:

DETENTION ROOM

STUDENT _____ DATE _____

TEACHER _____ AMOUNT OF TIME_____

WORK TO BE DONE _____

TIME IN	TIME OUT	
		SUPERVISOR'S SIGNATURE

COMMENTS:

Discipline Record Sheet

At the end of the day record information on students who misbehave.

STUDENT'S NAME	DATE	RULE BROKEN	CONSEQUENCES PROVIDED, NEGATIVE AND POSITIVE

Assertive Discipline

Pink Slip

Pink Slips are used to monitor misbehavior throughout the school.

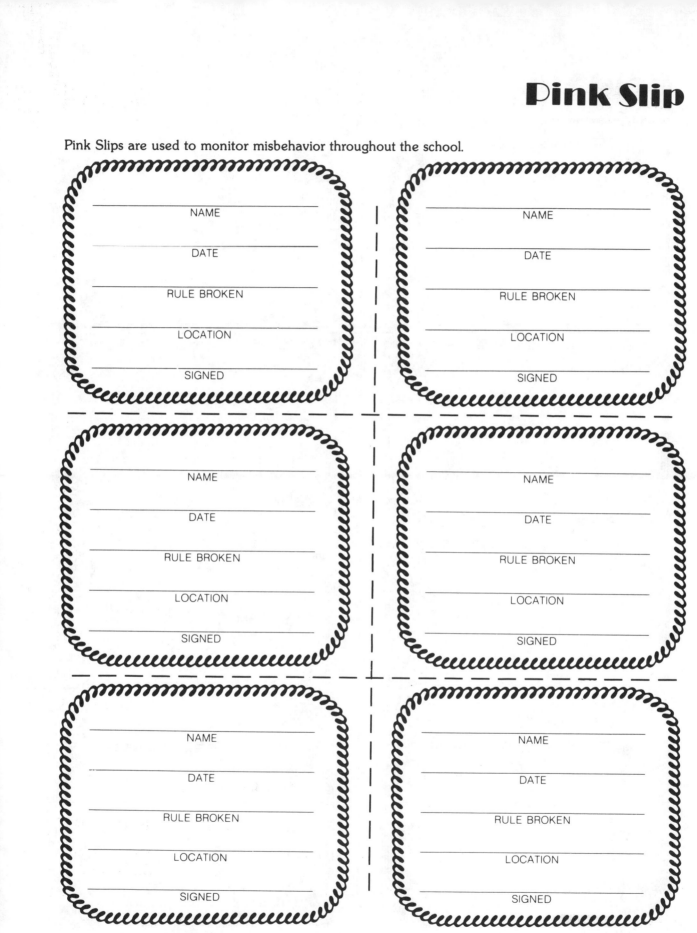

Gold Slip

Gold Slips are used to monitor appropriate behavior.

DATE _____

NAME _____
COMMENDABLE
BEHAVIOR _____

_____

LOCATION _____
SIGNED _____

DATE _____

NAME _____
COMMENDABLE
BEHAVIOR _____

LOCATION _____
SIGNED _____

DATE _____

NAME _____
COMMENDABLE
BEHAVIOR _____

_____

LOCATION _____
SIGNED _____

DATE _____

NAME _____
COMMENDABLE
BEHAVIOR _____

_____

LOCATION _____
SIGNED _____

DATE _____

NAME _____
COMMENDABLE
BEHAVIOR _____

_____

LOCATION _____
SIGNED _____

DATE _____

NAME _____
COMMENDABLE
BEHAVIOR _____

_____

LOCATION _____
SIGNED _____

DATE _____

NAME _____
COMMENDABLE
BEHAVIOR _____

_____

LOCATION _____
SIGNED _____

DATE _____

NAME _____
COMMENDABLE
BEHAVIOR _____

_____

LOCATION _____
SIGNED _____

Assertive Discipline

The great majority of students want to be in a safe, orderly, constructive environment.

SECTION THREE

How to Develop a Schoolwide Assertive Discipline Plan

The goal in developing a Schoolwide Discipline Plan is to have a systematic, consistent way in which to deal with discipline problems throughout the school. A Schoolwide Discipline Plan will create a positive and orderly environment so that students will have a maximum opportunity to learn.

Initiate Your Plan

A Schoolwide Discipline Plan will teach students that there are standards of behavior throughout the school and that they are expected to behave under the supervision of all adults, not only their classroom teachers. An effective Schoolwide Discipline Plan requires a two-sided effort from the staff:

1. Every teacher must have a Classroom Discipline Plan, i.e., a set of rules and consequences that are in effect at all times in each classroom. (See Section One.)

2. There must also be a Schoolwide Discipline Plan that governs student behavior in the common areas in the school, i.e., the playground, the lunchroom, or wherever the students are present without their classroom teacher.

Set Up a Committee

The development of a Schoolwide Discipline Plan should be the responsibility of a committee made up of the principal and teachers representing different grade levels. Those staff members chosen should be committed to making a positive change in the overall environment of the school.

Committee Responsibilities

The committee should use this checklist to help them develop a Schoolwide Discipline Plan.

- ☐ Establish schoolwide rules. (See pages 65-67.)

- ☐ Determine schoolwide disciplinary consequences. (See pages 68-69.)

- ☐ Organize the consequences and establish a system for monitoring student behavior. (See pages 69-71.)

- ☐ Determine schoolwide positive reinforcement. (See page 74.)

- ☐ Develop a system for monitoring appropriate student behavior. (See pages 75-76.)

- ☐ Present the rough draft of the Schoolwide Discipline Plan to the entire staff for feedback and input.

- ☐ Use the feedback from the staff to write a final version of the plan.

- ☐ Once the final version is approved, send a letter to parents from the principal explaining the plan in detail. (See page 80.)

- ☐ Before it is put into effect, the principal presents the Schoolwide Discipline Plan to the entire student body.

Establish Schoolwide Behavior Rules

First, the committee should discuss the problems that occur in the common areas of the school. They should then formulate general rules designed to stop all of the undesirable behaviors in these areas.

When developing a Schoolwide Discipline Plan, the committee members should keep in mind the importance of adapting different rules to different age levels. For example, in the playground, first-graders may be restricted from areas that sixth-graders have permission to occupy. Likewise, kindergarten students may not have the liberty of going out to the playground after lunch unescorted by a teacher, whereas older students may be allowed to do so.

Examples   General Schoolwide Rules

- Follow directions the first time they are given.
- Stay in assigned areas.
- Keep hands, feet and objects to yourself.
- No name calling, cussing or teasing.
- Use playground equipment appropriately.

- Students will follow directions the first time they are given.
- Students will not litter anywhere in or around the school.
- Students will not call each other names, or cuss or tease each other.
- Students will not write on or damage the school's or another person's property.
- Students will not fight.

The committee may feel that there are areas in the school that need specific rules. Such areas may include the hallway, the lunchroom, the playground and the auditorium.

Examples   Specific Area Rules
Lunchroom
- Follow directions the first time they are given.
- Do not throw food.
- Put all trash into the proper cans.
- When waiting in line to be served, keep hands, feet and objects to yourself.

Playground
- Follow directions the first time they are given.
- Use equipment according to the rules.
- No fighting.
- Stay within playground boundaries.
- Use appropriate language.

The committee may find it necessary to develop a separate tardy and/or absence policy. Pertinent rules may be:
- Be in your classsroom before the second bell rings.
- Bring a note from parents whenever you are absent.
- When entering the building after the beginning of school, you must first report to the office.

Establishing schoolwide behavior rules will set standards throughout the school. Students will know that they are expected to behave in an appropriate manner both in their classroom and on the school grounds.

Assertive Discipline

Schoolwide Discipline Rules

List the general schoolwide rules:

1. _____
2. _____
3. _____
4. _____
5. _____

List rules for specific areas:

Hallway

_____

_____

_____

Playground

_____

_____

_____

Lunchroom

_____

_____

_____

Restrooms

_____

_____

_____

Auditorium

_____

_____

_____

Other

_____

_____

_____

Determine Schoolwide Disciplinary Consequences

Choosing Consequences

Once the committee has set the rules, they must decide how to deal with students who break the schoolwide rules. As in the guidelines for the classroom plan, disciplinary consequences should be something the students do not like, but are in no way harmful or degrading to them. The consequences should be arranged in order of severity, constituting a discipline hierarchy.

Example   Schoolwide Discipline Hierarchy

1st time student breaks rule	=	Benched for remainder of recess period
2nd time student breaks rule	=	Benched for next two recess periods
3rd time student breaks rule	=	Benched for next two recess periods, parents called
4th time student breaks rule	=	Benched for one week of recess periods, parents called
5th time student breaks rule	=	Benched for one week of recess periods, office contacted, meeting scheduled with principal, teacher and parents

There are many consequences that can be used as part of your hierarchy. Be sure to choose consequences with which you are comfortable.

Examples   Schoolwide Disciplinary Consequences
- Loss of recess
- Yard clean-up
- After-school detention
- Call parents
- Parent conference
- Loss of lunchroom privileges
- Send to principal

An immediate and more severe consequence (severe clause) should be determined for blatant misbehavior such as fighting, stealing, using drugs, or defying authority. Severe consequences may be:
- Immediately send student to principal and contact parents
- In-school suspension (see page 71)

Organizing Consequences

Some of the consequences that the committee may choose to initiate will require discussion and planning. A special room or area may need to be set aside, paperwork and forms developed, and staff members may be asked to volunteer their services. Once the logistics for your particular school are agreed upon, write down the guidelines for each consequence and post the schedules of staff responsibilities in the office. To help you set up specific schoolwide consequences, the following pages list some of the general guidelines you need to follow.

Detention Room

A detention room or area is any room or part of a room designated as such for use before school, during lunch, during recess or after school.

Guidelines
- The room is staffed on a rotating basis by administrators, teachers or aides.
- The disruptive student is assigned a specific amount of time to spend in the room.
- Students do academic work in the detention room.
- Staff members may not talk with or counsel students while they are serving detention.
- The staff member in charge is given a list of all students who are assigned detention and checks off the names of those who did or did not serve detention.
- If a student does not appear, he or she receives double detention the next day or more severe consequences (for example, in-school suspension).
- If the student talks or disrupts in the detention room in any manner, he or she will be assigned extra detention and/or more severe consequences.
- Parents should be notified of detention.
- All teachers must volunteer time to supervise the detention room. Those who do not volunteer may not have the privilege of sending disruptive students there.

Detention Room Form

DETENTION ROOM

STUDENT __JENNIFER SCOTT__ DATE __11/23__

TEACHER __MRS. SCHILLING__ AMOUNT OF TIME __½ HOUR__

WORK TO BE DONE __SPELLING ASSIGNMENT, MATH WORKSHEET__

TIME IN	TIME OUT	
3⁰⁰ PM	3³⁰ PM	*E. Whitley*
		SUPERVISOR'S SIGNATURE

COMMENTS:

Jennifer worked quietly and completed both assignments.

Instructions

1. Teacher fills out form in duplicate.

2. One copy is sent to office. One copy is kept for teacher's files.

3. Student is escorted to detention room at specified time (recess, lunch, after school).

4. Supervisor in detention room fills out form and checks off student's name on master list.

5. Supervisor returns completed form to teacher after detention has been served.

6. Parents should be notified before student is to be detained after school.

In-School Suspension

In-school suspension is the disciplinary action of removing a student from a scheduled class and placing him or her in an isolated, closely-supervised environment. This consequence is generally used when the principal has become involved with a severely disruptive student. Those students attending in-school suspension are required to do work assigned by their teacher. In-school suspension is an alternative disciplinary action to placing students on out-of-school suspension. Since some students view spending a day at home preferable to being in school, especially if their parents are not home to supervise them, in-school suspension can be a more effective consequence.

Guidelines

- The room is well ventilated and well lighted. (If a room is not available, some schools set aside a desk in the main office or in the principal's office.)
- The room is monitored by an administrator, aide or other responsible adult.
- The student does academic work in silence.
- If the student disrupts in the in-school suspension room, he or she earns extra hours there.
- The student eats lunch alone, and is escorted to and from the restroom.
- The student remains in the room for a maximum of one day.
- If the student misbehaves after returning to the classroom, he or she must be sent again to the in-school suspension room.
- Parents must be notified that a student received in-school suspension.

The two most effective consequences for severe misbehavior are detention and in-school suspension. If your system is well organized and you follow the above guidelines, these two techniques will help to dramatically reduce discipline problems.

Emergency Situations

A method for removing severely disruptive students should be planned ahead of time. As a staff, decide who, in the absence of the principal, will be summoned in the event that an emergency arises. That person may be a teacher, an aide, custodian, etc.

Monitoring Student Behavior

Having decided the consequences, the committee should discuss a system for monitoring student misbehavior in all of the common areas in the school.

The use of Pink Slips is a very effective monitoring system. When a student misbehaves, the adult in charge records the student's name, date, rule broken, and location in the school of the infraction of the rule. (See sample, page 57.) This Pink Slip should be written in duplicate. When an older child misbehaves, the adult hands one copy to the child and turns the other copy in to the office. When a younger child misbehaves, the adult in charge simply tells the student that the misbehavior is being recorded. No slip is given to the child; however, a copy is turned over to the office. During the last period of the day, office personnel should go through the slips and indicate on a master list the consequences each disruptive student will receive. If a computer is available, it can be used for keeping track of Pink Slips. Consequences should be carried out the same day, or as soon as possible thereafter. Consequences should be cumulative over a marking period. That is, if a student disrupts three times in a marking period, that student receives the third consequence on the hierarchy, not three warnings.

The monitoring system and disciplinary consequences you choose should be tailored to the needs of your school. For example: In a small school, a Pink Slip system and discipline hierarchy may not be necessary. It may work well to send a disruptive student immediately to the office to be disciplined by the principal. On the other hand, in a large school with severe problems it may be necessary to utilize an elaborate monitoring system.

Remember, every time a student breaks a rule, a disciplinary consequence should be provided.

Linda Frazer
NAME

3/21
DATE

Littering
RULE BROKEN

Playground
LOCATION

B. Sanders
SIGNED

Assertive Discipline

# Disciplinary Consequences

List the consequences your school will provide for infractions of the schoolwide rules:

1st time _____

2nd time _____

3rd time _____

4th time _____

5th time _____

Severe Clause: _____

_____

List the consequences for tardies (if separate from general plan):

1st tardy _____

2nd tardy _____

3rd tardy _____

4th tardy _____

5th tardy _____

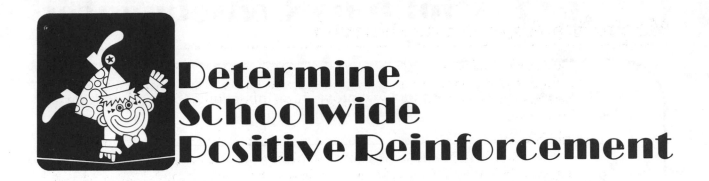

Determine Schoolwide Positive Reinforcement

As in the classroom plan the schoolwide plan must provide a balance between positive and negative reinforcement. A varied and consistent program of positive reinforcement will create a school that is an exciting place to be.

Choosing Positives

Your positive program should change frequently in order to continually motivate students to behave, and to continually reinforce those students who do behave appropriately. The positive reinforcement that your school uses can be chosen by the committee who develops the Schoolwide Discipline Plan, or a special Positive Committee can be formed to help in the selection of the rewards. The Positive Committee might include:

> Student council members
> Teachers
> PTA/PTO members
> Students who deserve special recognition

Examples   Schoolwide Positive Reinforcement
- Fast food coupons
- Discounts at local stores (record shop, bicycle shop)
- Letters home from principal
- Field trips
- Movies, cartoons, puppet shows
- Special luncheons
- Class banners
- Special assemblies
- Awards

Monitoring Appropriate Behavior

Just as the committee will choose numerous types of rewards to keep students motivated, they should also plan to use a variety of approaches for monitoring appropriate behavior. There are a number of ways of keeping track of and rewarding students who behave appropriately.

Gold Slip System. This system is effective for recognizing the good behavior of individual students throughout the school. Teachers, administrators, or aides who are on duty in the playground or lunchroom should fill out Gold Slips as they "catch students being good." (See page 58.) The Gold Slip is handed to the student who turns it over to the classroom teacher. With younger children, the student is told that he or she is getting a Gold Slip, and the adult who fills it out deposits it in a central location in the office. At the end of the month or grading period, the school can:

- Hold a Drawing. At a special assembly of the entire school (or entire grade in larger schools) a predetermined number of Gold Slips are drawn. The winners receive small gifts like pens, markers, books, gift certificates, or fast-food coupons.
- Count the Gold Slips. Every week an assigned student or office personnel counts the slips and tallies the number of points by grade level. At the end of a designated period of time, the grade level with the most points receives a special reward (field trip, film, luncheon).
- Send Home Certificates. In smaller schools, positive notes or certificates can be sent home for all students who received a certain number of Gold Slips.

Point System. This system is effective in motivating an entire class to behave. In the yard, gym, or cafeteria display a chart listing each class. (In larger schools one chart per grade level may be needed.) When the entire class behaves (first class to line up when bell rings, cleanest table after lunch, etc.), they receive points on the chart. This system is effective because it stimulates competition among classes.

Every month, or at the end of the grading period, the class or classes with the most points are recognized. The recognition can take many forms:

- Students may receive awards at a special assembly.
- Winners may see a film, go on an outing, etc.
- Classes may receive a special banner or blue ribbon to display on their door or bulletin board.

Remember, the students should be notified ahead of time how the Gold Slips or points will be used to reward them. If they are working towards a goal, they need to know it. If they need a certain number of points, they need to know that too.

Schoolwide Positive Reinforcement

List the schoolwide rewards.

Principal's Responsibilities

The following are guidelines for the principal to use when implementing a Schoolwide Discipline Plan.

See that each teacher has a Classroom Discipline Plan.

Evaluate and approve the Classroom Discipline Plan of each teacher.

Discuss with teachers what will occur if a student is sent to the office from the classroom.

Take the lead in organizing a Schoolwide Discipline Plan.

Set up a committee to write the plan.

Send a letter to parents. (See page 80.)

Speak with the student body regarding the plan.

Take the lead in modifying the plan as needed.

Supervise the implementation of the plan in the yard, lunchroom, halls, etc.

Train aides, teachers and other personnel in how to implement the plan.

Monitor the common areas of the school to make sure the rules are enforced consistently.

Take the lead in assuring that positive consequences are provided for students who behave.

Establish a plan for students sent to the office for disciplinary reasons.

When a student has repeatedly disregarded the rules or has exhibited severe misbehavior, he or she will be sent to the principal. It is important that the principal determine ahead of time how a student will be disciplined when sent to the office.

For example:

At the end of each visit to the office, the student should be told what will occur if he or she, by misbehaving, chooses to return.

A card should be kept for each student who comes to the office. The record should contain:

```
Student's name
Date
Why student was sent
What action principal took
What will occur if student returns
```

A card should be kept for each student who comes to the office. Such records will help the principal decide on the appropriate discipline action. The record should contain:

1st time to principal	= Discussion with student, parent conference, or in-school suspension
2nd time	= Parent conference and/or in-school suspension.
3rd time and all other times	= In-school suspension, out-of-school suspension

Establish positive consequences to be provided for students.

For example:

Principal's award (see page 50)
Positive note to parents (see page 81)
Special privileges

Provide back-up support for staff members.

Set up a plan to assist teachers in removing severely disruptive students from classrooms.
Aid teachers in establishing behavior contracts
Support teachers who are dealing with parents of problem students.

Supervise your teachers' implementation of the Classroom Discipline Plan.
Observe teachers and give constructive feedback:

> ☐ Does the teacher clearly tell students what he or she wants?
> ☐ Does the teacher provide positive reinforcement consistently?
> ☐ Does the teacher provide a negative consequence — name on board, etc. — every time a student disrupts or does not follow directions?
> ☐ If the teacher's plan is not effective, does he or she modify it to make it work better?

Positively support your teachers.
Teachers need positive support, too. Principals should recognize teachers who are consistent and successful in their discipline efforts. Positive support of your staff can be in the form of:

> Positive notes and letters
> Free periods
> Excused yard or cafeteria duty
> Small gifts (coffee mug, flowers, pen, book)

At each staff meeting, discuss discipline problems and how the entire staff can work together to improve them.

Letter from the Principal

Ridgewood Elementary School

201 Main Street   Phoenix, Arizona

Dear Parents:

The entire staff of Ridgewood Elementary School has the goal of establishing an atmosphere throughout the school in which children will feel safe, secure, and happy and, in addition, have a maximum opportunity to learn.

In an effort to accomplish this goal, we have developed a Schoolwide Assertive Discipline Plan. The plan specifies rules that cover the behaviors we expect from our students. The plan also states that students who break the rules will receive negative consequences, and students who follow the rules will receive positive consequences.

Our schoolwide rules are:
1. Follow directions the first time they are given.
2. No fighting, cussing or teasing.
3. Play in assigned areas only.
4. Do not litter or abuse school property.
4. Walk, don't run.

Students who disobey the rules will receive a Pink Slip. More than one Pink Slip means a student will lose time from recess. If your child receives four Pink Slips you will be asked to come to school to confer with the principal.

Students who follow the rules will receive Gold Slips. Once a month a special assembly will be held and prizes will be awarded to Gold Slip recipients.

Each teacher has a similar plan for classroom behavior, a copy of which will be sent to you by your child's teacher.

We are confident that such clearly stated and thorough Schoolwide and Classroom Assertive Discipline Plans will teach our children to be responsible for their actions and make this school year a positive and motivating experience.

We ask for your complete support in our efforts. Please discuss this letter with your child, then sign and return the bottom portion to school.

Sincerely,

Principal

- -

I have read and agree to support the Schoolwide Assertive Discipline Plan of Ridgewood Elementary School.

Parent's Signature _____ Date _____

Child's Name _____ Class _____

Comments _____

_____

Positive Notes from Principal

From the desk of
John D. Seyfang
PRINCIPAL

Walnut Street
Elementary School

Dear Parents:

I am pleased to tell you that your son's behavior has improved tremendously. For two weeks now, he has done all of his classwork and has not received one pink slip on the playground.

I appreciate how cooperative you have been in working with him at home. Thank you for your support.

Sincerely,

John D Seyfang

Principal

Sample Schoolwide Discipline Plan

Playground Rules
1. Follow directions the first time they are given.
2. Play in designated areas only.
3. Use playground equipment appropriately.
4. Do not fight.
5. No cussing or teasing.

Lunchroom Rules
1. Follow directions the first time they are given.
2. Speak in soft voices. Do not yell.
3. Do not throw food.
4. Walk, don't run.
5. Clean up your space after eating.

Consequences
Hand out Pink Slips to students who misbehave.

1 Pink Slip	=	Warning
2 Pink Slips	=	Loss of playground privileges for next day
3 Pink Slips	=	Loss of playground privileges for next three days
4 Pink Slips	=	Loss of playground privileges for one week, parents called
Severe Clause	=	Loss of playground privileges for one week, parent/teacher/ principal conference

Rewards
Individual students who behave will receive Gold Slips. A chart will hang in the lunchroom, and the classes who follow the rules will be recorded on the chart each day. There will be a drawing at a special assembly every 10 weeks. Students whose names are drawn will receive special privileges or small gifts.

Tardy Policy

1st tardy	= 15 minutes after school, parents called
2nd tardy	= 30 minutes after school, parents called
3rd tardy	= 30 minutes after school, parent/teacher conference
4th tardy	= Parent/teacher/principal conference

Notes

MATERIALS AVAILABLE FROM LEE CANTER & ASSOCIATES

Product #	Item Description	Unit Price
CA1009	Assertive Discipline for Parents	$ 7.95
CA1010	Parent Resource Guide	7.95
CA1016	Assertive Discipline Text	7.95
CA1019	Resource Materials Workbook—Secondary	7.95
CA1024	Resource Materials Workbook—Elementary	7.95
CA1026	Teacher's Mailbox	5.95
CA1033	Desktop Motivators—Monthly Positive Activities (gr. 1-4)	4.95
CA1034	Awards for Reinforcing Positive Behavior—Primary	4.95
CA1035	Awards for Reinforcing Positive Behavior—Intermediate	4.95
CA1036	Summer Motivators (available March '88)	4.95
CA1037	Fall Motivators	4.95
CA1038	Winter Motivators	4.95
CA1039	Spring Motivators	4.95
CA1040	Assertive Discipline Teacher Kit—Elementary	49.95
CA1041	Assertive Discipline Teacher Kit—Secondary	49.95
CA1042	Bulletin Boards for Reinforcing Positive Behavior—Primary	7.95
CA1043	Bulletin Boards for Reinforcing Positive Behavior—Intermediate	7.95
CA1048	Positive Reinforcement Activities—Elementary	5.95
CA1049	Parent Conference Book	6.95
CA1052	Positive Reinforcement Activities—Secondary	5.95
CA1053	Schoolwide Positive Activities	8.95
CA1063	Teacher's Plan Book Plus #2	4.95
CA1064	Teacher's Plan Book Plus	4.95
CA1071	Wanted for Good Behavior Poster	3.50
CA1072	Star Tracks Positive Reinforcement Poster—Intermediate	3.50
CA1073	Classroom Rules Poster—Primary	2.25
CA1074	Classroom Rules Poster—Intermediate	2.25
CA1075	We're on the Right Track Positive Reinforcement Poster—Primary	3.50
CA1076	Marbles-in-a-Jar Reward Poster (includes 150 marble stickers)	4.95
CA1083	"I'm an Assertive Teacher" Tote Bag	7.95
CA1085	"I'm an Assertive Teacher" Mug	4.95
CA1205	Homework Without Tears for Parents	7.95

Order from your local school supply dealer.

For more information about materials, in-service workshops and college courses, or to order a catalog, call Lee Canter and Associates, 800-262-4347. In California call 213-395-3221.